Shugo Chara Chan! 3

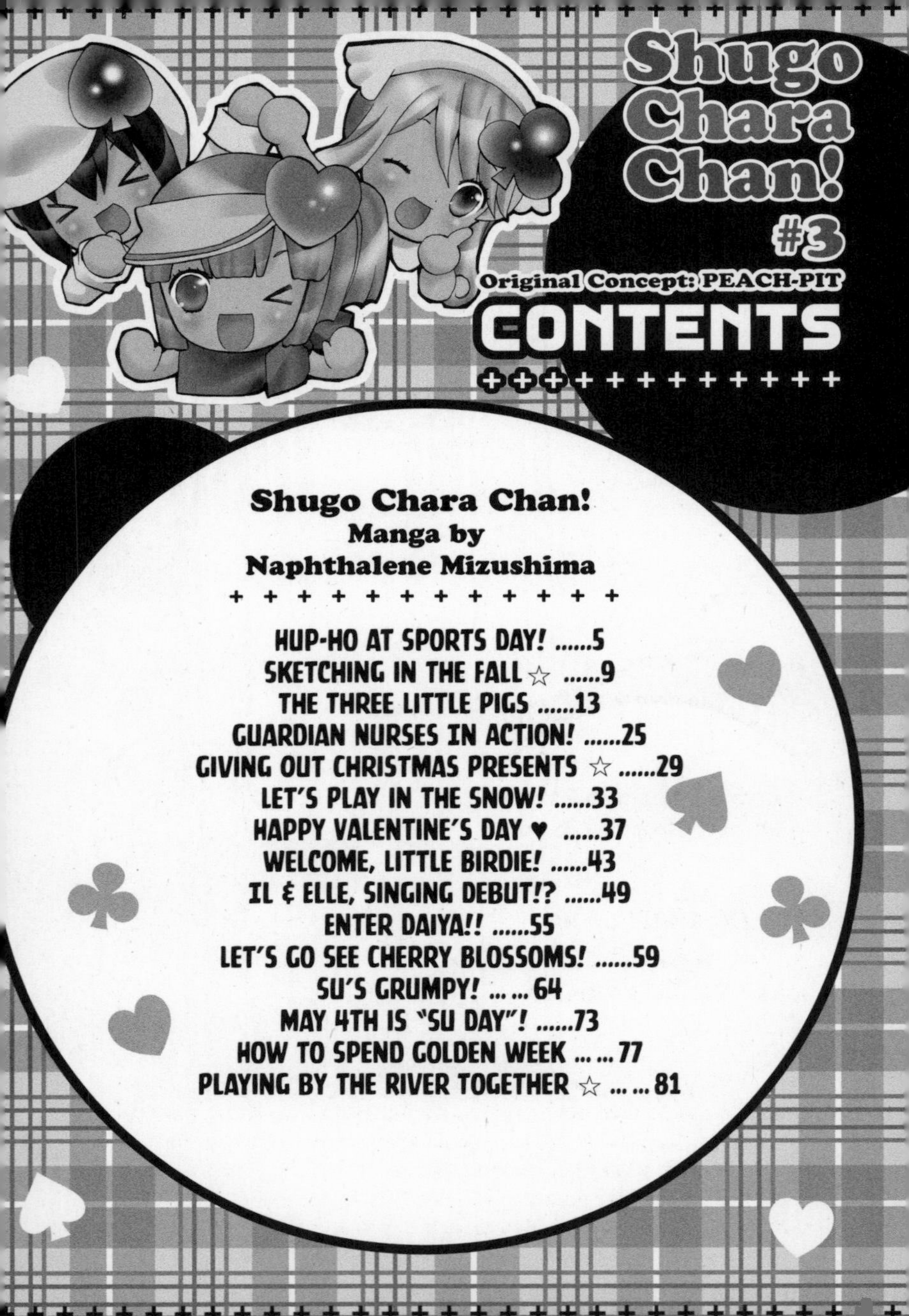

Shugo Chara Chan! #3

Original Concept: PEACH-PIT

CONTENTS

Shugo Chara Chan!
Manga by
Naphthalene Mizushima

HUP-HO AT SPORTS DAY! 5
SKETCHING IN THE FALL ☆ 9
THE THREE LITTLE PIGS 13
GUARDIAN NURSES IN ACTION! 25
GIVING OUT CHRISTMAS PRESENTS ☆ 29
LET'S PLAY IN THE SNOW! 33
HAPPY VALENTINE'S DAY ♥ 37
WELCOME, LITTLE BIRDIE! 43
IL & ELLE, SINGING DEBUT!? 49
ENTER DAIYA!! 55
LET'S GO SEE CHERRY BLOSSOMS! 59
SU'S GRUMPY! 64
MAY 4TH IS "SU DAY"! 73
HOW TO SPEND GOLDEN WEEK 77
PLAYING BY THE RIVER TOGETHER ☆ 81

Shugo Chara Chan! Festival 87

Manga by Naphthalene Mizushima

+ + + + + + + + + + + + + + + +

WANKOROBEE AND SHUGO CHARA CHAN! 90
MANGA BY YURIKO ABE

SHUGO CHARA CHAN! AND MäRCHEN-CHAN 92
MANGA BY SAKYO

DO XX TO SHUGO CHARA CHAN!? 96
MANGA BY EMA TOYAMA

SHUGO CHARA CHAN! IN "HELL GIRL" 98
MANGA BY MIYUKI ETO
ORIGINAL STORY/ BY HELL GIRL PROJECT

Special Manga Extra Shugo Chara Chan!

+ + + + + + + + + +

GO AROUND THE WORLD! 108

MANGA BY NAPHTHALENE MIZUSHIMA

"Guardian Characters" are versions of yourself you wish you could be. They hatch from eggs when children like you wish they could be someone else. Ran, Miki, and Su are the Guardian Characters of Amu-chan, an awesome but kind-of-snobby elementary school girl. There's something fun going on everyday for these tiny, upbeat girls! Come take a peek!!

FALL EDITION STARTS
ON THE NEXT PAGE!

NAPHTHALENE MIZUSHIMA
Shugo Chara Chan!
HUP-HO AT SPORTS DAY!
It's only natural the prince should be number one!
She's so co
I'm so hungry...
1
2
3
Hey every- one! Let's g to Sports Day! ★
Well... I guess it would be good to get some exercise.
I guess we have no choice.
Okay then! Let's split up into red and white teams!
Red? White!? We need a cool blue team!
What about a fresh green team!?
I shouldn't have both- ered...

Su-Style Race for the Bun

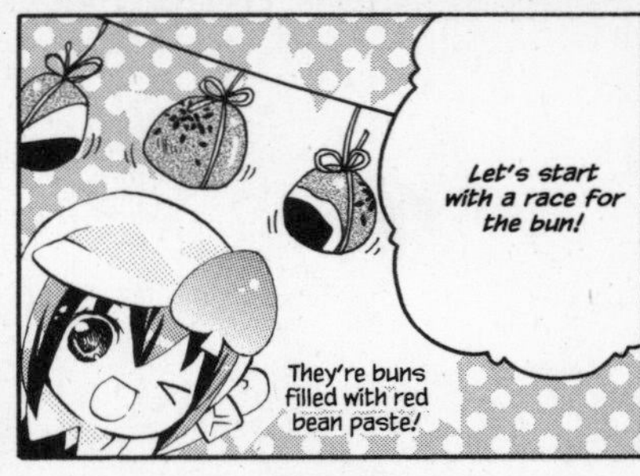

Let's start with a race for the bun!
They're buns filled with red bean paste!

I'm gonna win!
No, I am!

Huh!?
What happened to the buns?

No one beats me in an all-you-can-eat contest!!
That's not what we're playing!

Ranking Doesn't Matter ♬

Race for the bun do-over!
No way I'm losing to Su!

And... Go!
ダッシュ!
DASH!
She's so fast!

But look, I won!
1
Wait... where's Su!?

I realized that last time I was being rude, so this time I'm sitting down to eat. ♬
MUNCH MUNCH
Now she's having a picnic!?

Too Many Legs

Next is the three-legged race!
We're close! ♪

I want to play.
What? Why?
Everyone should be able to play.

But how?

Now it's a *five-legged* race...
Oh... I see...
1 2 3 4 5

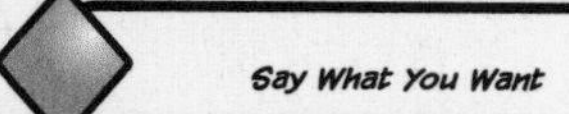
Say What You Want

It's time for the rolling ball!

I wonder if I have a big ball...?

How about this? ♫
Wh-...! That's my egg!

It's so hard to roll.
It's because the personality of its owner isn't very *well-rounded.*
What!? That's unfair!
ガビーン
SHOCK

No Need for Rules

The last game is the ball-toss!

Everyone, try to get the ball in this net!

あわわわ
Awawawah!
It's so high!

ワハハ
This is a piece of cake! ★
You're not al-lowed to fly!!

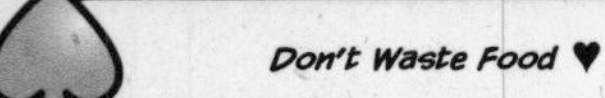

Don't Waste Food ♥

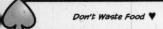

TIRED
I sure am hungry after all those sports!

Here you go, lunch! ♬
Wow! ♥♥

むぎゅ…
SQUISH...

There were some buns left over. ♥
After all you ate... I can't believe you can eat more...

Shugo Chara Chan!

SKETCHING IN THE FALL ★

Let's go sketch in the park! ♬

Why not? It's nice outside!

Let's sketch "Fall things!"
Alright!

ROLL ROLL

...What are all those things?

Stuff that fell off the desk this morning.
Not that kind of Fall!

Fall Reminds Me Of...

Fall reminds me of mackerel!

HMMMM
The shape... It's so hard to capture.

And the color... it's like a mix between black and blue.
We have to use shiny colored pencils.
HMMMM
STINK
...Maybe we shouldn't have used a raw one...
Yeah ...

Mackerel ABCs

I grilled it! ♬

I can't... It smells so delicious...
I can't concentrate on my sketch!

In that case ...
...let's draw this mackerel!
THUD!
MACKEREL SPLIT AND BROILED SOY SAUCE FLAVOR

There's nothing Fall-like about canned mackerel!
I don't want to eat it or sketch it!

Falling Leaves Remind Me Of...
The falling leaves are so pretty!
I'm gonna draw these next!
WHEEE
CRUNCH
WHISP
ZOOOOOO!!
In That Case!
Su has wings!?
WOW
She looks like a fairy.
She's the perfect model!!
SCRATCH SCRATCH SCRATCH
YOU'RE A BIT HEAVY...
A dragon-fly!?
Help... I'm being kid-napped...!

Everyone's Enthusiastic

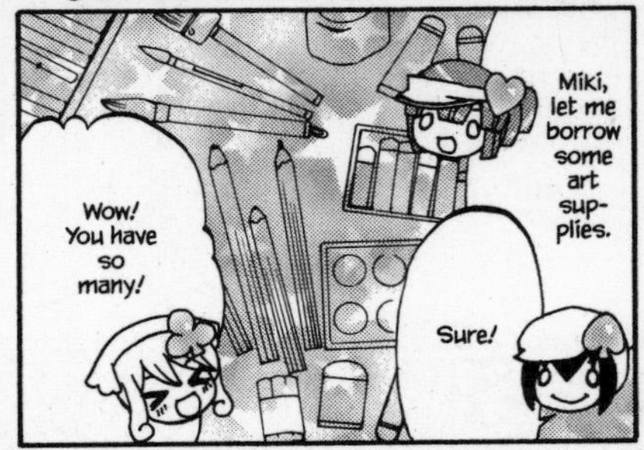
Miki, let me borrow some art supplies.
Sure!
Wow! You have so many!

This would work great as a baton!
I love the red color ♥
SWIRL
SWIRL

This would be great for getting dust out of the corners!
SWEEP SWEEP

Don't play with art supplies!
We're serious!
We're not playing
Serious about cleaning!
Serious about cheering!

Smells Great

Huh?
You have some bread here.
It's a bit dirty.

Miki, you're such a gourmand.
Heh-heh
むふふ
No!
スゥにいわれたくないし

I use that bread instead of an eraser...
...for charcoal drawings!

I knew the smell reminded me of a delicious charcoal-grill! ♥
Why do you eat everything!?

Art in the Fall!
The Guardian Character play is about to start!! ★
Shugo Chara Chan!
The Three Little Pigs
They're putting on "The Three Little Pigs"!
This is the story of the Three Little Pigs
The little pigs built houses out of straw, wood, and bricks.
The straw and wood house...
...were blown down by a wolf who wanted to eat the little pigs.
But the brick house was safe.
"Sturdy"
Until...

The wolf tried to get into the house through the chimney.
But the little pigs boiled a big pot of water under the chimney and waited...
The wolf fell into the pot, and ran away. And that was that!
So now for the play!
YAY!
I made my house out of straw!
Role of oldest brother: Ran
Oh...?

...It looks more like a bird's nest to me...
Perfect for my egg! ♥
I bet you gave up in the middle of building it.
He-he. How'd you know?
Doing the same thing over and over again is so boring.
This house is so easy! I don't even have to blow it down! ♥♥
I'M GONNA EAT YOU!
Role of wolf: Yoru
EEEK!
You have a point...

A wooden house?
Role of middle brother : Su
Since chopping down trees is bad for the earth... ♥
...I built a house out of candy!
WOW!
GASP
I get to eat both a main dish (Su) and dessert! Two birds with one stone! ♬
Oh no! This was a perfect house for the wolf!!
I've got to remake my house out of something the wolf doesn't eat!

Ta-d
It's an onion house!
Since onions transform the hemoglobin in red blood cells...
...and decrease the red blood cell count...
...cats and dogs aren't allowed to eat them!!
STOMP
Argh... There's nothing I can do...!
But
But you're just standing there.
You're not in the house.
Oh please. Like there's any way...
...I could live in a stinky onion house!
No Way Jose
In that case... I'm gonna eat you!
EEEK!
キャアアアア

So the last house, mine...
Role of Youngest Brother: Miki
Is a fancy designer apartment...
... with exposed brick!
How about it?
Great job, Miki! It's so artistic!
They were bitten
And it looks so sturdy too!
This looks like it could be trouble!
STUMPED

According to the story, I'm supposed to go in through th. chimney...
...Huh?
Fancy designer apartments these days don't have chimneys...!!
ガーン
WHAAAAT
At this rate, the story's going to end here...
What should we do?
I know!
We just to make a little renova-tion. ★
Anything's possible, isn't it?
CLINK CLANK CLANK
Here we go!

Okay! We need to boil some water before the wolf comes in.
Let's get back at that wolf!
ドス
FLOP
ぼっちゃん
KER-SPLASH
EEEEK!!
He he he... It's hot, isn't it?
We won't forgive you even if you surrender.
.....
He's so rprised he an't even speak.

That was a nice bath!
ザパ
STEAM
What!?
He's right.
It's about 104 degrees.
This *is* really nice.
It's because he fell before his cue.
Let's put in some bathwater scent!
SPLISH

And so, in the end, the three little pigs and the wolf all enjoyed a nice bath together.
All's well that ends well.
It's a little cramped.
おーー!!
WOO HOO!!
CHEER CHEER
It was... *okay.*
They showed up↓
Hey!!
What are you doing in my room!?
There's water all over the floor!!!
EEEEK!
We're sorry!
Looks like it didn't end so well after all...

Shugo Chara Chan! ONE - PANEL MANGA ☆

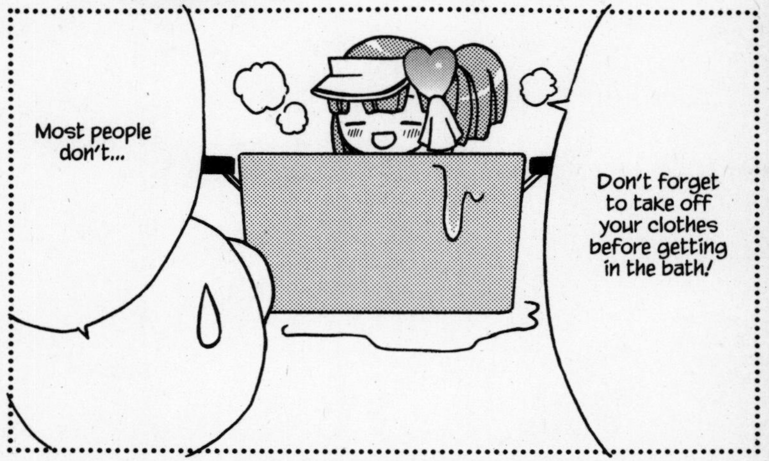
Don't forget to take off your clothes before getting in the bath!
Most people don't...

WINTER EDITION STARTS ON
THE NEXT PAGE!

Shugo Chara Chan!
GUARDIAN NURSES IN ACTION
Hey guys...
...I don't feel so good.
There!
Where ...?
Whoa!
You're burning up.
CLINK
We've got to cool her down!!
えいっ!!
That'll cool her down too much!!
Fridge

More Harm or Help...?

Let's cool down her head with some ice.

Ooh, so cool...
That feels nice...

But since you went to all this trouble, it would have been nice to freeze some juice instead.

That way, I could drink it after it melted. ♥
LICK
Your face would get all sticky!
Ants would come!

Wanna Play Dress-Up?

She's sweating a lot. We should change her clothes.
HMMM

Let's borrow some clothes from Amu-chan's dolls!
Which one would you like, Su?
FLING

They're all kinda costume-y...
Whoa. This one has wings...
Does it have to be one of these?

The Patient's Request

Let us know if you need anything, okay?
Really?

I'd really like some pudding...
Let me check in the refrigerator.

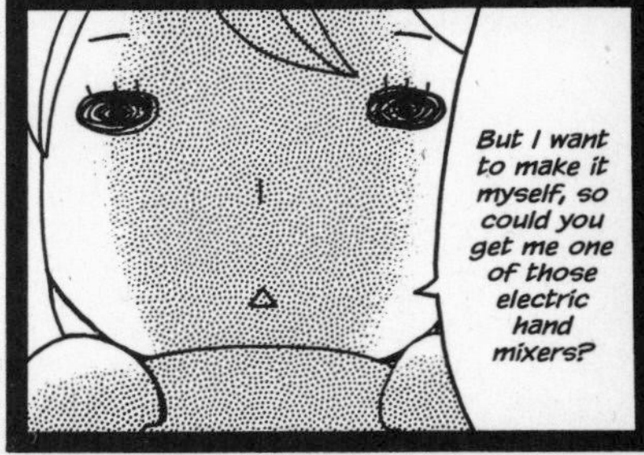

But I want to make it myself, so could you get me one of those electric hand mixers?

And also one of those rice pressure cookers!!
They're really popular these days.
How about you just take the pudding!?
Wow, there's lots of stuff I want too. Maybe I should get sick...

Balance

I found some boil-in-the-bag rice porridge!
国産米使用
しろがゆ
レンジでいっぷん
Shirogame
Contains Domestically Grown Rice
1 Minute in the Microwave

Since a teacup is too big for us, let's pour it into a sake cup...
Contents 100g

And an umeboshi plum*...
... to make it a balanced meal!

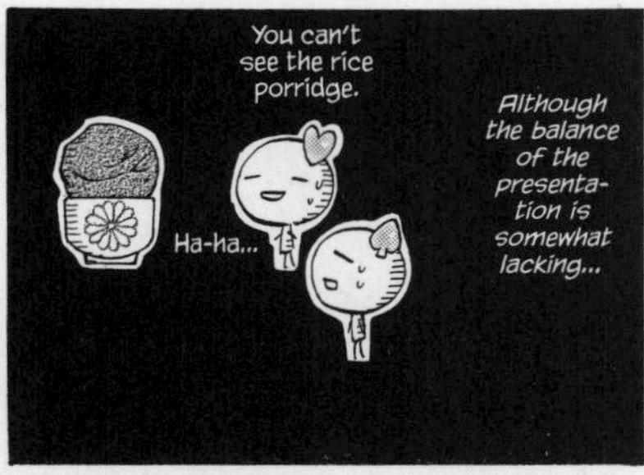

Although the balance of the presentation is somewhat lacking...
You can't see the rice porridge.
Ha-ha...

*A small pickled plum usually served as a side for rice. Considered to fight bacteria and indigestion. Very salty and sour.

Losing Control

She must be bored sleeping all the time.
Why don't I read her a book?

Once upon a time, somewhere far away...
I wanna see the pictures too!
Turn it this way please.

No problem!
HUP-HO
よっこらしょ
Once upon a time
Somewhere far away

Take Care!

Thanks to you guys, I feel a lot better now!
Awesome!

If either of you ever gets sick, I'll take really good care of you!
Thank you!

...
<Sneeze>

Whoops.
Eeeek!
A- Already!?
I must have caught yours...
Both of you at once!?
<Sneeze>

Shugo Chara Chan!
GIVING OUT CHRISTMAS PRESENTS
This year, we're gonna give out Christmas presents...
...to all the Guardian Characters!
But we don't know where they all live.
Is there some way to search for them?
Hmm. A search, huh...?
Oh!
I know!
Is she gonna appear in this manga?
Hrm?
The nearest station is...
CLICK
Cell Phone
Searching online!?

Keeping Warm

I see. So we have to dress up as Santa.
Who's gonna be the reindeer?
So...

No way. I don't want to wear that.
It offends my artistic sensibility.
None of us wanna wear it!

Okay! I'll wear it!!
えっ!?
Huh!?
You're okay with it?

This outfit is much warmer than dressing up as Santa! ♥ ♥
It's cause Ran gets cold so easily.
SNUGGLE

Mistaken Judgment

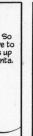

Hey! What do you guys think you're doing?
?

We have to sneak into their houses at night to deliver the presents.
If you dress like you always do, it'll ruin the illusion!!

Sneak in...
At night...

So you're saying we should dress in dark colors so they don't notice us?
Not like burglars!!

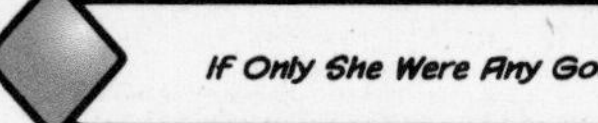
If Only She Were Any Good...

Really...?

What do I want...?

How about a song...?
!

What? You want me to write you a song!?
That will help me grow as an artist!
I'll do the backup dance!

No no... I want you to *listen to me sing* a song!!
HOWL
I've never heard of a participa-tory Christmas present!!

So I asked everyone what they wanted for Christmas! ♫
メモ

I want a ducky like in my dreams...

That moves by itself...
...and is just big enough for me to ride!!
WOBBLE
トコトコ

I'm thinking a real duck is perfect.
Even though it's gonna get big really soon.
QUACK
Great.

How exciting! Meow!

I want a big fish!

But I bet he wouldn't really want a raw fish by his pillow.
So we got him some dried bonito flakes instead.
That's a good idea!

He wants a whole tuna or something!!
That's asking for too much!
スピー
SNORE

A Blessed Nuisance?

We're finally done giving out everyone's presents!
Phew
ガラッ
SLIDE
Now that you mention it, we didn't get any presents for ourselves.

!!
A pile of presents!?

They must have delivered them while we were away...
じぃーん
SIGH
I'm so happy!

But...
...now we have nowhere to sleep.
むぎゅっ
SQUISH
Yeah...

Shugo Chara Chan!
Let's Play in the Snow!
Woo-hoo! It snowed!
Look, she's making something already.
A snowball!?
むぎゅぅ
PRESS PRESS
No!
Can't you tell?
It's a soft round rice cake stuffed with sweet bean jam!
How is anyone sup-posed to know that!?

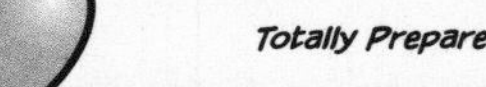
Totally Prepared

Let's make snow sculptures!
Since there's so much snow on the ground.

I bet if we make a base first, we can form the shape with a spoon.

Just like eating gelato! ♥
Don't eat the sculpture.

It's fine! I put a heat cloth on my tummy so it won't get cold!
No need to worry.
You thought this through, didn't you?

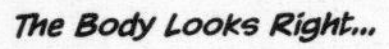
The Body Looks Right...

I've only made snowmen before...
A snow sculpture sounds kinda hard.

Wait a sec
What's the difference between a snow sculpture and a snowman anyway?

Just think of it as anything besides a snowman!
Don't think too hard!

How about this sculpture of Su?
THUD
Of Su!?
Huh!?
Think a little harder next time!!

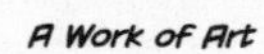

A Work of Art

Wow, look at Miki!
Gotta use a toothpick for these details...

Hers really does look a sculpture!
Awesome!
Like Venus de Milo or Michelangelo's David?

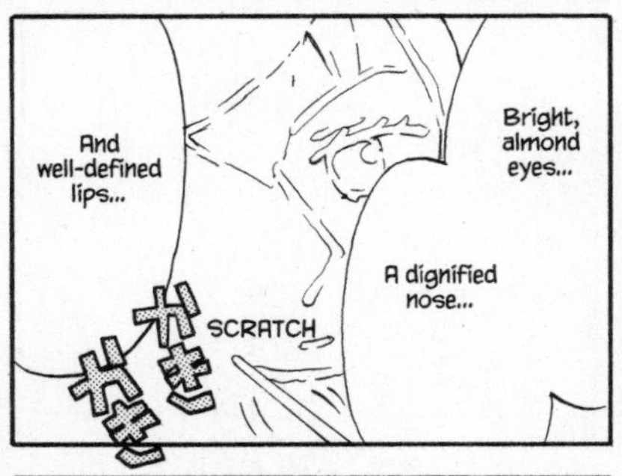
Bright, almond eyes...
A dignified nose...
And well-defined lips...
SCRATCH

Looks just like me!!
I can see how getting carried away like that would be fun.

I Guess So...

But I really worked hard to make it beautiful!
Oh yeah? Like how?

Hmm? Can't you tell?
No.

I used beautiful white snow!!

....
I guess the snow is kinda beauti-ful...

The Ideal Home

Let's build an igloo to keep warm!

"Igloo" is just the word for "house" in the north, right?
Err... Actually
It's...
In that case ...

I want a spiral staircase between the first and second floors!!
I want a kitchen with induction heating and lots of storage!

FLOP
Why do you never listen?
I'll use you as the base for a snow sculpture!
Run away
Eeek! We're sorry!!

All Together

So this is an igloo!

All of us together, hidden in the snow...
It's like a secret base!
WHEE

A secret, huh...

Whenever I hear a secret, I always want to tell people!
SQUEEZE
Don't you think you told a few too many people!?
SQUEEZE

Shugo Chara Chan!

Happy Valent

Happy Valentine's Day ♥

Today's Valentine's Day! ★

Who out of the Guardian Characters would you give a chocolate to?

What about you, Miki?

Definitely Kiseki!

I would give one to Daichi! We both like to have fun!
I guess I'd give one to Musashi. He looks like he can make good traditional Japanese food!
WOO-HOO
This is not a cooking knife!
Because I could expect the most from him in return!
People call him the King after all...
You're so modern, Miki.

Not Punny
I wish my chocolate could tell a story.
Heh-heh... Leave that to me! ♬

Ta-da!
White Chocolate
A dog?

You see? A tail!!

"Tell a story"... "Tell a tale"...
とりゃ
Not funny at all!!!

A Prank

Look! Look! Mine came out really well! ♥
Heart
Wow! It did!

How did she manage...?
Slightly jealous
But it seems a little... plain. Can I decorate it?
With a pastry pen.

This kind of shape really looks good with sharp and defined lines!
Wow...!

All done. ♥
You're so mean!!

Just What It Looks Like

Hints of Curry

This time I made a chocolate that will really get you going! ♫

I'd like...

...to make chocolate that's a little different!

ちょこん

PLUNK

This shape...

You know how some people add hints of chocolate to their curry?

Is it a kiss chocolate?
Nope!
Well how about adding hints of curry to our chocolate?

TA-DA
I just covered some raw garlic with chocolate! ★
Whoa! That'll really boost your stamina!!
You'd take a bite, and delicious curry would come oozing out...
CLENCH
That's not a "hint"!!
That's just chocolate with curry inside.

Hard At Work

I have a calling to make an artistic chocolate!

I'm going to carve this chocolate block like a sculpture!

Yikes... It's starting to melt...
But I must... In the name of art!

Which one is the chocolate!?
Totally Covered!

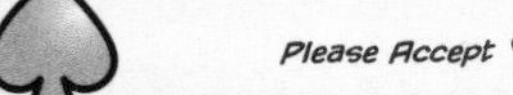
Please Accept ♥

Whoa... Amu-chan got so much chocolate, even though she's a girl!
She's popular among girls too, because she's so cool and aloof.

Even though we made some chocolate for her...
She probably won't want it...
しゅん...
TEE-HEE

Oh no!
I'd love to try it!

Well then, here you go!!
Are these your failed attempts!?

Shugo Chara Chan! ONE - PANEL MANGA ☆

A chocolate fondue sure looks like a big chocolate bath...
STEP...
SHOCK
ゴクリ
She's gonna go in!
ぐつ
BUBBLE
ぐつ
BUBBLE

Shugo Chara Chan!
ONE - PANEL MANGA ☆
And how could I resist a cheese fondue...?
You'll get burned in both of them!
STEP...
BUBBLE
BUBBLE

Shugo Chara Chan!

Welcome, Little Birdie!

タイヘン!

Oh No!

A baby bird fell out of his nest!

TWEET

I don't see the mother anywhere, so let's take care of him!

A round one, out of twigs and branches.

Are sticks okay too?

At home
SHAKE SHAKE
We should make a nest for him!

She's using candy sticks!?
It's hard to make them round...
The nest will melt!!

Feeding

びぃー
TWEET TWEET
びぃぃ
Do you suppose he's hungry?

⬆ Miki made a real nest!

It says here...
HOW TO RAISE BIRDS
A HANDBOOK

..."they put their beaks in their mothers' throats and feed directly from their mothers' stomachs."

I did just have a snack...
GLURP
ぐえっ
I just can't.
うっ...

It Is a Bean...

Beans are one of birds' favorite things to eat!

He's still a baby, so he can't eat one yet.

That's right.
It has to be something soft!

Soft beans...
Not natto*!?

*Fermented soy beans.

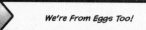

Keep Trying!

Would you like some milk?
TWEET

It says to "warm milk in the human hand."
All right!
How to Feed Milk

Argh... It's so cold...!
We have to warm it...!

It's cause we don't have "human hands"!!

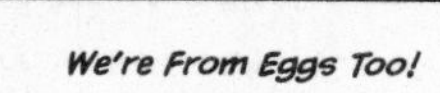
We're From Eggs Too!

<Yawn> I'm getting sleepy!

Let's go to bed.
We should all keep the birdie warm.

Let's all snuggle together...
Good night!

Just like a real bird's nest.

We're Supposed To Be Warm

We're supposed to keep him warm by holding him!

Okay!
HUG

Wow! He's so warm!
So soft and cuddly!

It's because he's covered 100% with feathers!!
We're the ones who are supposed to be keeping him warm.

Be Careful!

Several Days Later
Poppo (we named him) has gotten so big!

Po?
You think it's about time for him to leave the nest?
Let's help him practice flying!

Let's attach some balloons to him so he can see what it feels like to fly!
Flying high!

ZWOOSH
Argh! I brought too many balloons!!
You're the one flying high!

Equipped With Parachute

Should we just let him fly normally?
Come here, Poppo!

I'm kinda worried...
He'll be fine! I attached a parachute...

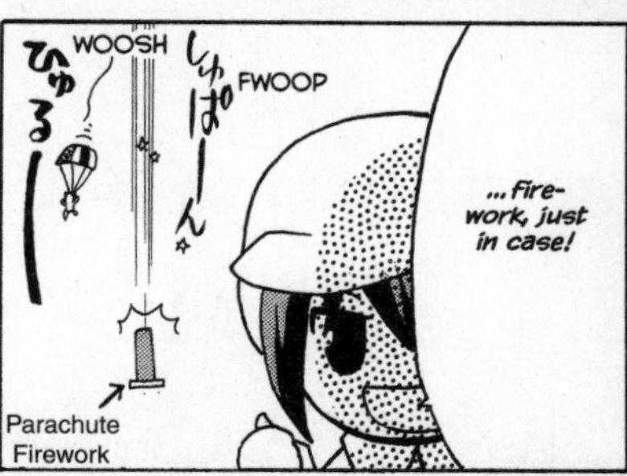
...fire-work, just in case!
FWOOP
しゅぱーん
WOOSH
ひゅるー
Parachute Firework

We'll light it in case he falls!
How's that going to help Poppo!?

He's Very Picky

Why don't we try coaxing him with food?

Here you go, Poppo...
It's a bean!
......

He won't come.
しゅん
SNIFF

Do you suppose he only eats high-grade, Tamba Province beans*...?
I don't think he's that fussy.

*Tamba is a province of northern Kyoto famous for its black beans.

What else can we do...?

HMMMM うーん

LOOK!

バッサ

FLAP

He's flying!?

This way, Poppo!

Is he leaving already?

スッ

FWISH

Oh!

His mother...

Good for him...

Yeah...

That Night

It's unlike you guys to sleep in here.

What happened?

We miss our down feather blanket!

Shugo Chara Chan!

Il & Elle, Singing Debut!?

We're going to debut as a singing duo!

We'll ask our manager to take care of the songs.

I wanna join too!
Huh?

Three-person performing groups are hot now, right?

We're not "performers." We're singers!!
ダブルツッコミ
Double Retort
はは...
HA HA...
The two of them are like a comedy duo already...

Temari's Talent
You're writing a song?
I'm good at writing poems.
An awesome rock song!
A pop song!
Get ready for it
Rock and roll forever dude
Feel it in your soul
So you write a haiku**, the shortest type of poem in the world!?
What a cool poem!
Oh! I forgot to add a word that evokes the season.
It is a poem though...
Ho-ho-ho!
KYUN
Stubborn
Since I'm an artist...
...it's easy for me to write lyrics and compose songs.
Thank you so much!
I know! I'll write an enka* song!
What!? Write an awesome rock song!!
I want a nice pop song!
Well then, let's compromise with an enka song.
How is that a compromise!?

*A music genre of slow ballads that resemble traditional Japanese music. Not considered very cool.

**Very short Japanese poetry form, usually consisting of three phrases, with 5, 7, and 5 syllables in each.

A Little Forced

Can you play an instrument?
Singing duos play the guitar and stuff, right?

It's a little retro, but I can play the air guitar! ★
SHAKA-SHAN
Awesome!!

Uh... Um...

I can play the air whistle!
PHHHHT
Not so awe-some!!

How About This?

I can also play the air castanets!
That's not very awesome, either.

What kind of air instru-ment...
...should I play...?

Ah-ha!

Since it's good at singing, I can air-sing!!
How is that different from lip-synching?
SMACK SMACK SMACK

Just What You Ordered

I'll take care of your outfits!
Do you have any requests?

Something black and white, that really stands out!!

Okay, done!
YANK

Pandas!?
I also have Malayan tapir and cow versions. ♬

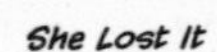

She Lost It

Leave the backup dancing to me! ★

Okay! Take these pom-pons.
What? These are so out of style.
They don't match the band image. Use something cooler!!

WHAM
OUT OF STYLE
NOT COOL AT ALL

Fine then. Why don't you hold these?
Go on!!
PRICK
PRICK
W- We're sorry...!
SOB

Shugo Chara Chan! ONE - PANEL MANGA ☆

Or you guys could dress up as sesame! ☆
Black Sesame
White Sesame
No way!!

SPRING EDITION STARTS ON THE NEXT PAGE!

Shugo Chara Chan!
ENTER DAIYA!!
April is the season of new encounters!
I wonder if we'll meet anyone?
I think you will!
TA-DA!
Daiya!?
What's with that outfit!?
I had a bad experience at a tanning salon once...
So now I'm being careful about ultraviolet rays.
That was from a tanning salon!?
From Her "Black Daiya" Period
I was young and reckless.
Ho-ho-ho

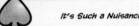

How Could You...

We've never really all been together before...
I'm a little nervous.
Just a little

Well, since we're going to hang out, let's shake hands...
Oh!
Hold on a sec!
すっ
Rustling Sound

Kills Germs
For Shiny Clean Hands!
RUB
ゴシ
RUB
ゴシ
RUB
ゴシ

What a snob!!
No!
My character is supposed to always be shining!!

It's Such a Nuisance!

Let's compliment her to break the ice.
Good idea!

Daiya, your hair is so long and pretty!
Thank you.

But taking care of it is such a nuisance...
Especially trying to blow dry it...

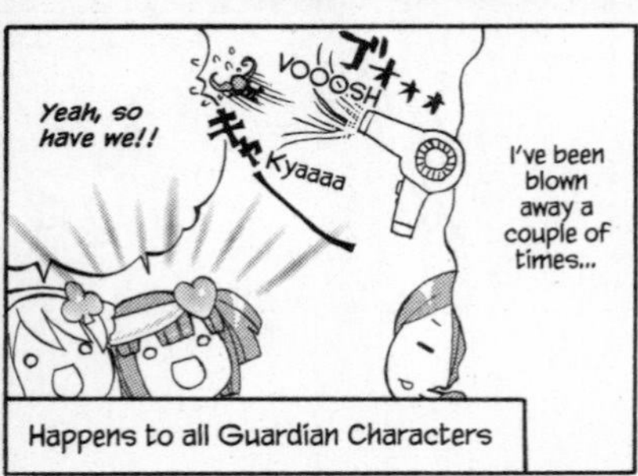
I've been blown away a couple of times...
ゴオォォ
VOOOSH
キャー
Kyaaaa
Yeah, so have we!!

Happens to all Guardian Characters

Hard to Read

I can never tell what Daiya is thinking.

Right now it looks like she's spacing out...

But maybe she's thinking all about her hopes and dreams...
How mysterious!

SPACE
Actually wasn't thinking about anything.

Shiny ♥

I love shiny things. ♥

The shiny stars!

Shiny jewels!

And shiny...
Kyaaa!
So you like anything shiny!?
WOW

Hidden Ability
There's nothing shiny about that person...
WHISPER ぼそっ
"I can see you're shining underneath...!"
He's wearing a wig!?
You have the ability to see through wigs!
Ho-ho-ho
That's Cheating
Eek!
Eek!
LURCH ガバッ
I'll be late!!
Don't worry Amu-chan!
Huh?
The path of the stars...
...can cut through time and space.
Come! Take the path of the stars to school!
Um...
You're not supposed to use your magic like that!!

Shugo Chara Chan!
Let's Go See Cherry Blossoms!
Let's go see the cherry blossoms together! ★
Whoa!
So many people!
There's nowhere to sit.
What about here?
What a great view! ♥
Good thing we're Guardian Charac-ters! ♬

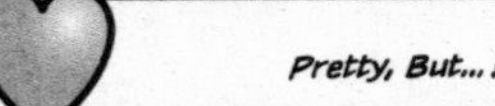
Pretty, But...!

ぶわっ
RUSTLE

The petals are so pretty as they fall! ♥

そわ
TWITCH
そわ...
TWITCH

The falling petals remind me of confetti, and I just have to clean them up!
It must be tough if you have OCD.

Fun, But...!

Ha-ha-ha!
Flower viewing is so much fun! ♬

Alright!
I'm gonna do the flower dance!

I made pompons out of petals. ♥
See?
ふぁさ〜
RUSTLE

Hey! It's shed-ding!
Can you please go over there!?
Sorry ...

Ran-bunctious

WHEE
WHEE
Ran's really having fun.

She's so excited to be here.
She's so wild and...

...Ran-bunctious!!

Hmph! That was really funny! ★
TEE HEE HEE
くすくす
You're the only one who thinks so.

Substitution

So beautiful...
I should sketch this...

No!
Instead...

Su, could you sit here for a sec?
You want me to sit on your sketchbook?

I'm gonna make a pressed flower! ♬
And you seem to be the heaviest!
What am I, a weight!?

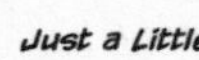

Changing One's Image

How do these blos-soms look ...
...as hair decora-tions?

Wow! They look great!
ホホホ
HO HO HO
Won-derful!

But since there are so many... ♥
...you should use more! ♬

TA-DA!
ドーン!!
It's a big pink afro!!
That's too many!

Just a Little

I added a pinch of salt and some hot water...
...and made cherry blos-som tea!

Smells great!
It warms you up.
The light pink color is cute too!
Amazing!

Can you put some in a bigger cup?
Wow, you really like it!

Wow, you really like it! ♥
Like a celebrity taking a bath in rose petals!
Don't bathe in the tea!

Shugo Chara Chan! ONE - PANEL MANGA ☆

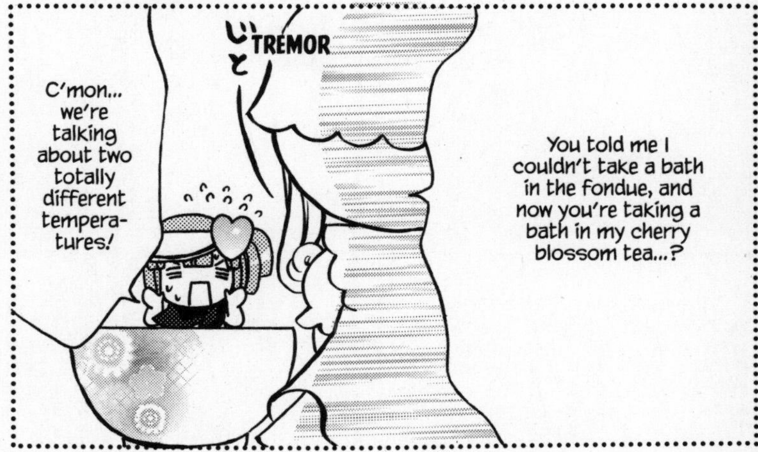
You told me I couldn't take a bath in the fondue, and now you're taking a bath in my cherry blossom tea...?
いと
TREMOR
C'mon... we're talking about two totally different tempera-tures!

Shugo Chara Chan!

Su's Grumpy!

It's true.
I like doing house-work!

No, no Su...
This is for your own good.

But look at you two!
Half-Eaten
Not Put Away
You're both so spoiled!!

You've gained some weight recently, so you should get exercise by cleaning this stuff up!
POINT
That's none of your busi-ness!

Strong Will

If you guys don't help me with the house-work...
...I refuse to do any-thing!

プイッ!
HMPH!

.....

Don't hold your breath!
You'll die! You'll die!
ぷぅ
uuu...

Already a Bad Girl?

Maybe if I looked a little scarier...
...they'd listen to me more!

Maybe I should dye my hair like a bad girl!
It's already dyed green.

In that case ... I'll get a perm!!

Oh. I already have an inward-curl perm...
She just noticed now...

Unknown Talent

I'm going to reinvent myself...
...as a scary older woman with flashy makeup!

Wow!
Su! You have a talent for makeup!!

......
Ha-ha-ha! Like a monster!
The dramatic kind.

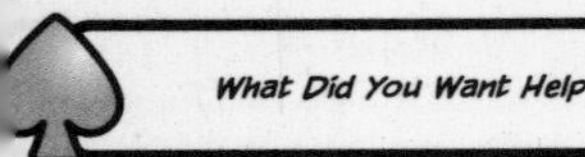

What Did You Want Help With?

It's our fault, so we should help her out a little.
Okay.

You should hold the mascara brush vertically!

You should be a little more condescending when you talk!

RAGE
I don't want help becoming scary...
...I want help with the housework!!

That's Not What It's For!

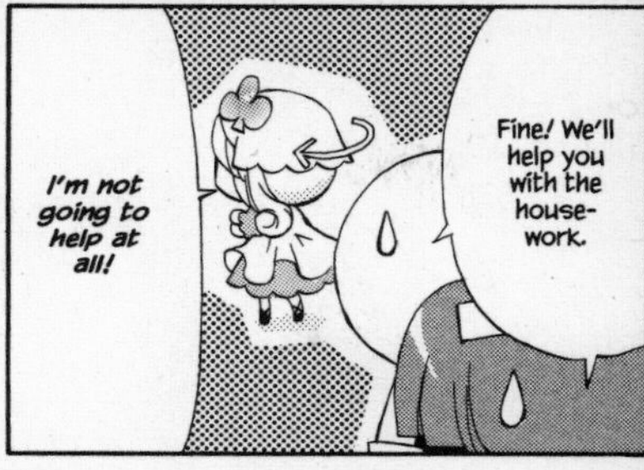

Fine! We'll help you with the house-work.
I'm not going to help at all!

Broom...
Broom...
キョロ
BLINK BLINK
キョロ
I wonder where it is.
Oh!

Lend me your pompon.
Huh?

Just put a stick on it, and it's a broom!
Looks like I have a talent for invention too!
Stop it!

Multipurpose!

Sweeping up is pretty tiring!

I know!
Another invention?

All we have to do is role up our Guardian eggs with scotch tape...
WITH THE STICKY SIDE ON THE OUTSIDE

...and roll it around to pick up all the dirt!♫
Eh
ゴロ
ROLL
ゴロ
ROLL
Be careful with your egg!

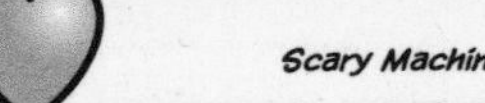
Scary Machine

It's impressive how Su always uses such old-fashioned cleaning methods.
Like a broom

It would be so much easier to use a vacuum cleaner.
True, but think of the size.

Something that big...

...means that we might be the ones who get cleaned up...
VOOOSH
You're right...

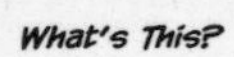
What's This?

I can't find a wash-cloth...!

Why don't you sew this white cloth together and make one?
Good idea!

...Hmm?
What are these folds...?

This is Su's hat!!
I'm sorry!!
IT WAS FOLDED SO NEATLY...

Useless

I poked myself with the needle.
Here's a bandage.
A bit too big...

Being a Guardian Character is a little inconvenient at times like these...
I CAN'T USE THIS...
Heh-heh...
Leave it to the King of Inven-tion!

じゃーーん!
TA-DA!

What, you just drew it on!?
I'm an artist by trade, after all!

Simple Sushi

キュッ
SQUEEZE
Why don't I try some cooking?

I'm gonna make sushi, a dish that requires a high level of skill!
That's a tough one to start out with!

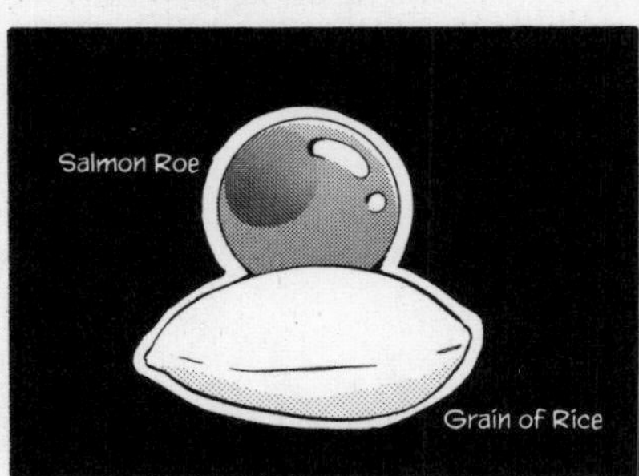
Salmon Roe
Grain of Rice

This is a perfect size for use to eat! ♫
So where's the "high level of skill"?

So have you realized how hard housework is?
Yes.
We'll help you out a little from now on.
Thanks! I'd appreciate that!
びしょ
SPLASH
We tried to help...
...but water got everyhere!
ガシャ
CRASH
We tried to help...
...but a plate broke in two!
ぐっちゃり...
SOB SOB...
Th-... That's fine!
You don't have to help anymore!
I guess we're just not cut out for house-work...
We didn't mean any harm...

Shugo Chara Chan! ONE - PANEL MANGA ☆

Here's an apron as a present for all your hard work! ♥
Another draw-ing!?
Did you just draw it on with a marker!?

Shugo Chara Chan! ONE - PANEL MANGA ☆

Being a housewife is hard.
You have to clean up after your bratty kids...
SIGH
ふう…
Don't call us bratty kids!

Shugo Chara Chan!

May 4th is "Su Day"!

Today's my big day, so I dressed up extra special! ♫
Heh-heh.
What's today's date?
It's May fourth...

Whoa! You have an extra row of frills!
What's going on!?

Oh! It's "Greenery Day*"!
Tee-hee ♥
I can't believe *that's* what you consider "dressing up"...

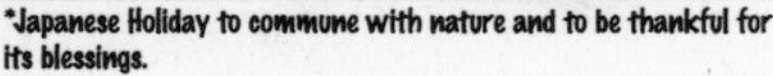
*Japanese Holiday to commune with nature and to be thankful for its blessings.

Wanna Try?

Let's celebrate Su Day together!
What do you have in mind?

Seems Cheap
Do we get our own days, too?
Blue and red, huh?

Why, a huge feast of course!

Blue Day...
Well, Marine Day* is kind of close!
Since the ocean is blue.

....
....

Red Day...
Hmm ...

If we cook, though, you might wish we hadn't...
I'll cook it myself!

It makes me think of the "All prices slashed!!" signs in supermarkets.
Don't make my day a sale!

*Japanese Holiday to show gratitude for the blessings of the oceans.

Adam and Eve
She Realized

Done celebrating Su
The real meaning of Greenery Day...
...is to enjoy and treasure nature.

Let's play with these leaves here!
Done dressing up

Look! I made a green dress with my leaf!
I just wrapped it!
Looks like she's enjoying nature.

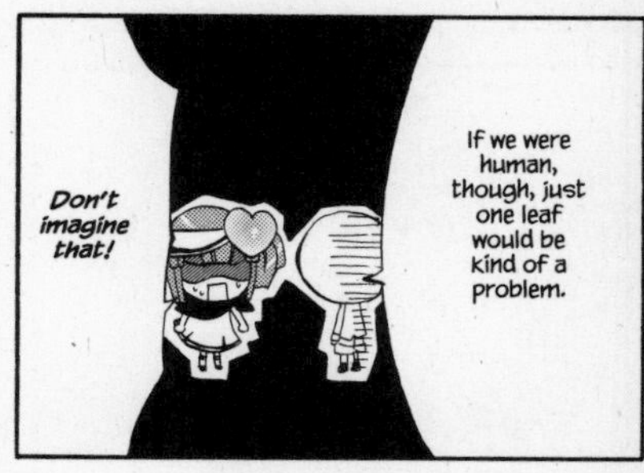

If we were human, though, just one leaf would be kind of a problem.
Don't imagine that!

PEER
Eeek!
There's a worm on the leaf!
Eeeeek!

It's a little hard to enjoy and treasure worms!

B-... But wait...
くね くね
WIGGLE
くね くね
WIGGLE
This movement...

HEE-HAW
It's a worm rodeo!
くね
WIGGLE
くね
WIGGLE
You're brave, Ran...
I couldn't do that

Rather Dangerous

ごくり…
SHIVER

Are these ...
...torture instru-ments?

No.
They're the spiked mountains of hell!

Cactus
シャキーン
GLEAM
Nature is scary!!

Miniature

In nature, there are oceans, rivers, and mountains.
But they're all so far away!

There's a mountain right there.
Really!?

You see?

It's a moun-tain...
...of broc-coli!

Shugo Chara Chan!
How to Spend Golden Week*
It's Golden Week! Let's go somewhere!
I can't. I have home-work.
Aww... C'mon!
PULL
Pulling my arm won't work.
Then we'll pull this!
HUP!
SNAP
Ouch! Did you just pull out a hair?
Stop it!!

* A period in late April and early May where there are seven Japanese holidays close together. A lot of people take vacations.

A Sandwich!
How about a picnic in the park, at least?
Hmm ...
We should make sand-wiches! ♪
What should we put in it?
Woo-hoo! This bread is so soft and fluffy! ♥
It feels so good!
FLOP
Hup!
One Ran sandwich, coming up! ★
キャー
Eeeek!
A New Sport
I wanna play frisbee at the park!
We'll all get on top...
Amu-chan will toss the frisbee...
And we'll see who can stay on the longest!
キャー EEEK
キャ EEEK
That's not how frisbee usually works.

A Prank

Let's help Amu-chan with her homework!
Maybe if she finishes early, she can take us somewhere!

But we don't really know much about studying...
I guess what we can do is...

Cheering!
Making snacks!
As for me...

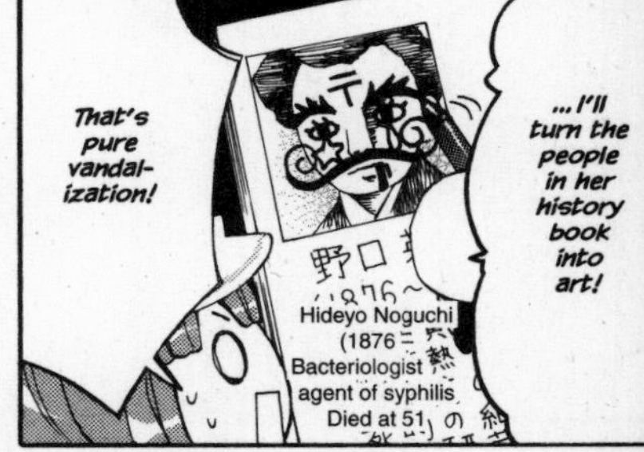

...I'll turn the people in her history book into art!
That's pure vandalization!
Hideyo Noguchi
(1876
Bacteriologist
agent of syphilis
Died at 51

No! We Understand!

Phew... I'm done.
Yay!

THUD
Hmm?

You were pretending to do homework, but really reading "Shugo Chara Chan!" Volume 3!?
Tee-hee
Sorry!

Oh no, we totally understand!
Knew you would...

Summer Edition
Starts on the Next
Page

Shugo Chara Chan!
Playing by the River Together ★
Amu-chan's going to play by the river with her family! ♪
The current in the river is strong, so you have to be careful.
OKAY
I'm gonna hold these strings down with a rock...
...and tie them around you!
Were we bad or something?
I just don't want you to get swept away...

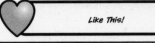

Like This!

ゆらり…
FLOAT
Wouldn't it be nice to float down the river in a toy bamboo boat?

But how do we make one?
Hmm ...

I know!
ポン
SMACK

Just standing on top of it is like surfing! How do I look?
Hmm... Not quite right...

She Ruined It

We did it!
We're floating! ♪

I'm gonna make your boat even cooler!!
What!?
I don't have a good feeling about this...
TA-DA

Here you go! ★

POP
ゆあぁぁぁ
ARRRGH
Don't poke a hole in it!
Water'll get in...

Smoke

They're having a barbeque by the river!
How wonderful!

もくもく
BILLOW
But the smoke ...!
ケホ ケホ
COUGH COUGH

Run, Miki!

It's so cool... Like a singer's performance!!
バーン
TA-DA
もくもくもく
BILLOW BILLOW

Not The Best Example

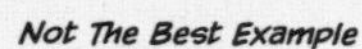

Argh!
Sparks are flying from the charcoal!
バチバチ
CRACKLE CRACKLE
Eeeek!

Can't you be a little more careful, Amu-chan?
There's nothing I can do...!

You don't understand how dangerous sparks are to us!
It would be like if...

...a giant fireball came flying at you!!
Since that's never happened to me, I can't say that I understand.

Tumble

Let's make ones small enough for us!
That looks good!
SIZZLE

Wow! ♥
Heh-he-he ♫

But it's too hot for us to get close...
Amu-chan, can you grill these?
Sure!

TUMBLE
Whoops!!
It fell through the grid!
This is real open-fire grilling!
SIZZLE
WAAAH

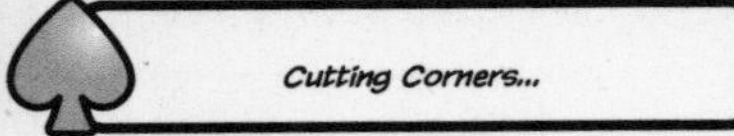
Cutting Corners...

Regular Size
SIZZLE
Cut
Stick on
All Done!
Why don't we just cut off pieces after they're grilled?

But this meat is really hot, and it looks hard to cut...
Is there anything else...?

Oh!
This could work really well! ♫

Just corn!?
What sad kabobs...
GRUMBLE

Shugo Chara Chan! ONE - PANEL MANGA ☆

This is the last one-panel manga in this volume!
But don't worry. The fun goes on! ★

Shugo Chara Chan Festival!
It Starts Now!

This is the third Shugo Chara Chan Festival!
We made a lot of friends from "Nakayo-shi"!
You go to all sorts of places...
Do you fly all the time to get there?
That must be tiring...
We sometimes take the train and the Shinkansen*!
I love the Green Cars**! ♪
That must get expensive for three people!
These guys... ride for free!!
Since they're invisible...

*Japan's high-speed trains, also known as "bullet trains."
**In Japan, first class cars are known as "Green Cars."

Let's have some fun!

NAKAYOSI
I ♥ NAKAYOSI
HARIO
Shugo Chara Chan!
FESTIVA

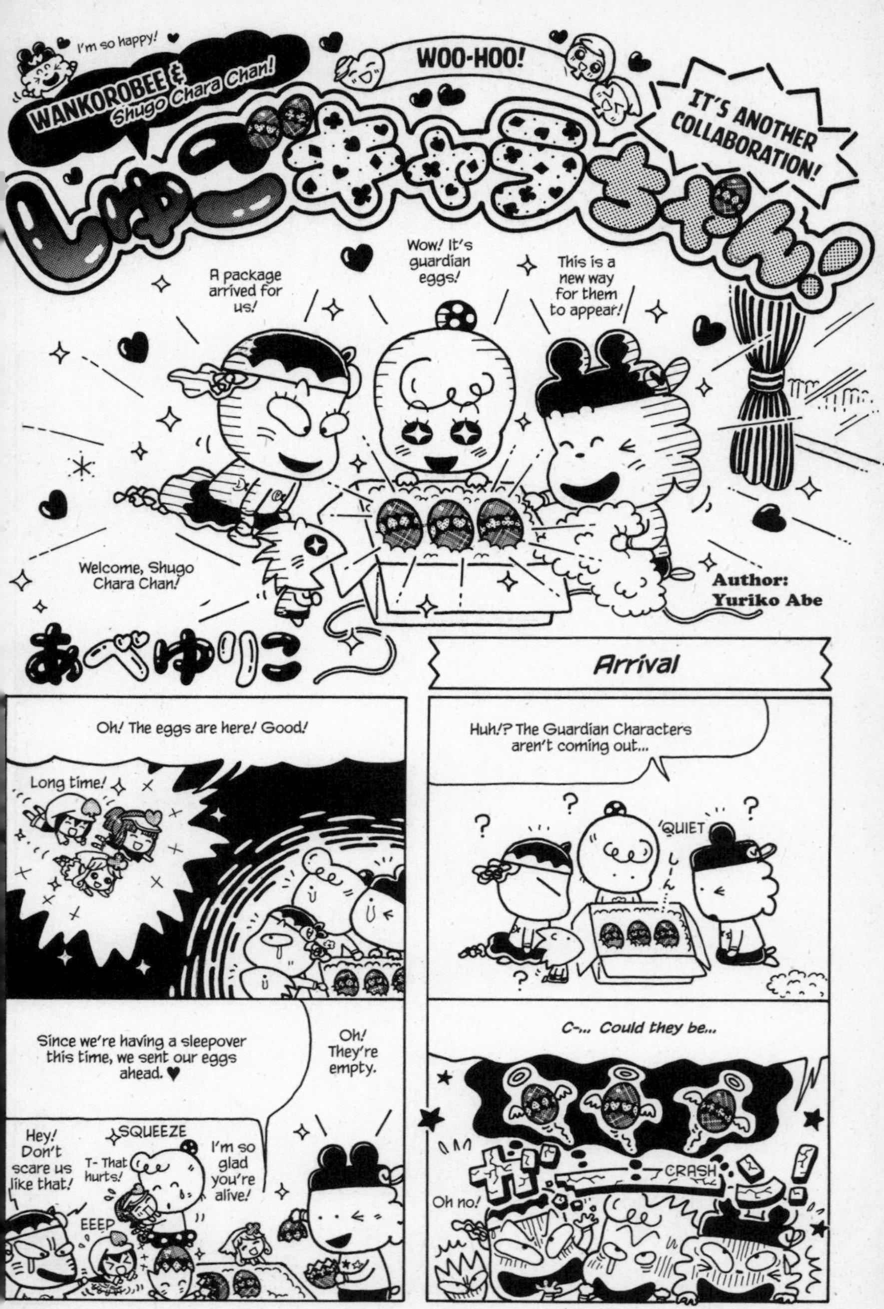

I'm so happy!
WANKOROBEE & Shugo Chara Chan!
WOO-HOO!
IT'S ANOTHER COLLABORATION!
A package arrived for us!
Wow! It's guardian eggs!
This is a new way for them to appear!
Welcome, Shugo Chara Chan!
Author: Yuriko Abe
あべゆりこ
Arrival
Oh! The eggs are here! Good!
Long time!
Huh!? The Guardian Characters aren't coming out...
QUIET
しーん
Since we're having a sleepover this time, we sent our eggs ahead. ♥
Oh! They're empty.
Hey! Don't scare us like that!
SQUEEZE
T- That hurts!
I'm so glad you're alive!
EEEP
C-... Could they be...
CRASH
Oh no!

Relax

Good morning, Guardian Characters! ♥

Nngh
ん一…

Wow! This looks great! ♥

Maybe we should stay at your house for a while, Shime-chan!

Sure! Stay as long as you want.
Let's tell Amu-chan!
Good idea!

I was wondering why you didn't come back... It was the food!

Wow! It's the real Amu-chan! Can I have your autograph?
Amu-chan came to find us.
WAN

Amu-chan, you should relax in this carefree world from time to time! ♫

That sounds nice!
Yay!
Don't take her away! She doesn't have time for this!
Editor of "Shugo Chara!"

Sleepover

Is this your house, Wankorobee?

Yup it is!
Make yourselves at home.

Shime-chan, take us to your house too!

What? That's fine, but...
Let's go! C'mon!
We wanna go to your house!

What's wrong with my house!?

SOB
ぐすっ

Well, you're technically a boy, Wankorobee, so we wouldn't want it to become a scandal!

Excellent
That's true!
"Technically"...!?
EEEK!

SAKYO
Shugo Chara Chan! x Märchen-chan
Give me your eyeball!
Okay! Sure!
ゴロン!! ROLL
If only she were more cheerful of a character!!
Hm...
I'll never get Date's eyeball at this rate...!
We'll help her reinvent her look!!
POP

Guardian Characters Arrive!!
Leave it to me, Ran, to make your friend into a cheerful, happy character!!
Lucky Ran gets all the lines!
R-... Really...!?
It's a deal!!
THUMP
I should do a character swap!?

With Ran...!?
That's right! You're going to act like Ran, Date! ♥
Let's do a character swap!
And then I'll get your eyeball!!!
Heh-heh-heh
But I...
ポッ
BLUSH
I've always wanted...
...to be like *Amu-chan.*
What?

And so
Date!
Give me your eyeball!!
...You've got to be kidding.
TURN
Note Date
BLUSH
I've always wanted to do that...
How was I?
Wig
I'm so happy for you...
What was that? So embar-rassing!!
It's good to be Amu-chan!
↑The real Amu-chan

Where are we now?
Six Flowers Private Junior High School
STOMP
GLARE
Huh?
E-... Eeeek!
DO XX TO SHUGO CHARA CHAN!?
Author: Ema Toyama
What are you?
GLOMP
We're... We're Guardian Characters!
TREMBLE
TREMBLE
What!? Fairies?
Ackk! That's cold!
I'm scared!
It seems I finally acquired the ability to see fairies...
Now how shall I use you...?
Is she gonna kill us!?
CLUCK CLUCK

Oh!
A nice-looking young man!
EEK EEK
You over there, help us!
Huh?
Who the hell are you? Pesky brats.
I'm tired as hell.
SNEER
This is the worst character type!
Shigure, these are fairies who will grant our wishes.
That's wrong!
Seriously?
I'm going to wish for the power to enter the word of books!
We can't do that!
WAAAH
This place is awful!
Oh!
Hmm?
FRESH BAKED MELLON BREAD
Here! Have some!
!!
In the end, they didn't mind this world.

* See "Shugo Chara Chan!" Volume 1
HELL GIRL 地獄少女
Shugo Chara Chan! IN
Manga/Miyuki Eto
Original Story/Hell Girl Project
Since we failed miserably to help Ai-chan change her image 2 volumes ago...
...this is our chance for vindication!
You came all the way to hell for that?
I'm so happy! ♥
WOOOOOO
What a scary smile!!
Leave smiling to me!!
I think that's the first problem...

The Jester of Hell!!
Stop!!
Character Transformation: Clown Drop
Why are you acting even scarier!?
Give her another character...!
Aw...!
There's not much difference between a demon and hell...
And I'm already 400 years old...
Just a little too young...
THUD
I know! Let's take a risk...
...and give you a character of the opposite personality!!

Character Transformation: Amulet Angel!!
What a nice smile!!
GRIN
Well then, I'm off to work.
GRIN GRIN
Good luck!!
...Huh?
By work, she means...
Sending people to hell...?
No way!!
Why should I go to hell!?
You're such a bad loser!
Mis-tress!!
Send this young man to...

!?
Mis-tress...!?
Why are you dressed like that...?
Pitiful shadow, wandering in darkness...
With nothing but contempt and hatred for humans...
A vexed soul, drowning in sin...
GRAB
HOW WOULD YOU LIKE TO DIE?
Mistress!!
He's not supposed to go to heaven!!!
....

Wankorobee Episode

We have to pack these eggs really well...
...so they don't crack on the way to Wankorobee's house!

Let's put a "Fragile" label on the box too.
STICK
FRAGILE

I don't know if that's enough...
Let's write some-thing too!

SCRIBBLE
かき かき
"Treat carefully, because the contents are fragile, just like your heart."
Well said!

Märchen-chan Episode

Maybe we're actually kind of like fairies after all!
We could be!
Do you think it's in the encyclopedia?

Does that mean that Amu-chan and all the Guardians who can see us...

Oh no!
Their eyeballs are in danger!!

We have to guard the Guardians!!
What's going on, guys?
POW!!

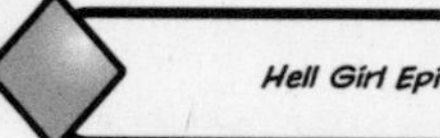

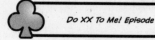

Hell Girl Episode

Elle, you played an important role!
Tee-hee-hee! ★

Maybe I can make some money from this smile, what do you think?
You're never satis-fied, are you?

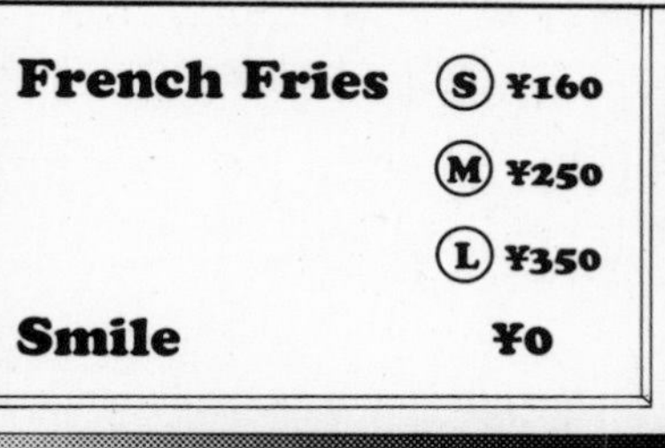
French Fries
S ¥160
M ¥250
L ¥350
Smile ¥0

...O Yen...?
It just means that people aren't stupid!
C'mon, smile!

Do XX To Me! Episode

I'm addicted to melon bread because of the one Akira-kun gave us!

I like eating the soft part on the inside first! ♥
Me too! ♥

It's like a cave now!
We can fit all the way in!

Seen from the other side ...
Woo-hoo! This is fun! ♬
The melon bread is talking!?
Amu-chan

We brought some presents back for you, Amu-chan! ♥
Shime-chan's hand-baked cookies!
Rabiko's fairy powder!
Glasses like the ones Yukina-chan wears!
And from Ai-chan...
Well, she said that this is all they have in hell...
Take that back right now!!
END

We've got some comments from the artists!
Thanks, everyone!!

COMMENT

The third co-performance!
Screen printing for Wankorobee is always detailed and usually I don't have to do it, so it was a little tough. But when it was done it felt really great, and I applauded myself. ♬
It was great having Amu-chan this time too…♥

YURIKO

Yuriko Abe

It was wonderful having a chance to visit the Shugo Chara Chan! world again!!
Well, I basically drew whatever I wanted to this time again. I hope it came out all right! (LOL)
I hope to keep showering the adorable Guardian Characters with as much love as I can!! Amore! ♥♥♥

Sakyo

My worlds usually don't have any fantasy, so it was fun to hang out with the Guardian Characters!
+ + + + + + + + + + + + + + + + +
Ema Toyama
Thanks for having me again! I worked hard on this episode again, and I really liked how the Clown Drop came out. It was really fun to draw. Oh, and I'm actually very clumsy, so I can't play jacks for my life.
+ + + + + + + + + + + + + + + + +
Miyuki Eto

America
Australia

SPECIAL MANGA EXTRA

Shugo Chara Chan!

GO AROUND THE WORLD!

France
Spain
Egypt

Ran In Spain

Spain

In Spain, they have...
...bull-fighting!

Look at how strong they are!
Very intimidating.

Uh...
Huh?
Is it coming after me!?
Be-cause you're red!
Run!

Miki in France

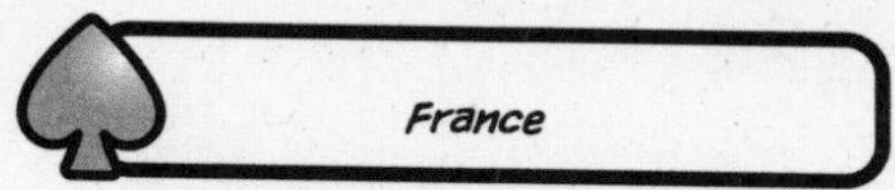
France

Paris is a city of art!
I hope to be inspired artistically here! ♥

Shugo Chara Chan!
Shugo Chara Chan!
10
Shugo Chara Chan!
Cosplay*

Somehow, everything seems very familiar...
It seems that Japanese anime and manga are very popular in France these days...
へえー

***A popular pastime in Japan and elsewhere involving dressing up as your favorite anime or manga characters.**

Su in America

America

Everything in America is super-sized!

Easily 6'5"!
They're huge!!

THUD
10 liters!
This would last a lifetime...

And the food too, of course!

So Su become super-sized...
Because of the food...

Daiya in Australia

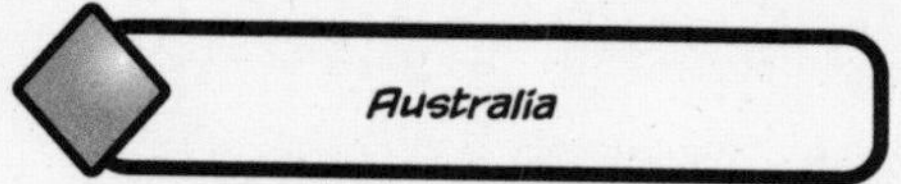
Australia

A lot of the world's diamonds come from Australia.
Wow! It's so shiny! ♥

キラーン
GLEAM
Oh!
That crow must be after my diamond because it's shiny!
What? Me?
Does this mean I'm even shinier than a diamond? ♥
It's probably just looking for dinner...

Yoro in Egypt

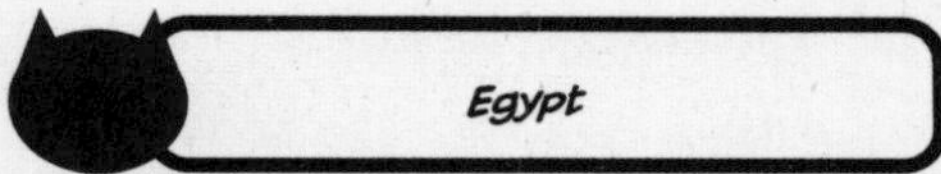
Egypt

Cats were once worshipped as gods in Egypt!
Come on! Worship me!!
....
しらんぷり
IGNORE

No one's worship-ping me!
It's probably because they can't see you...
Being a Guardian Character and all...

END

Make your own collaboration
with Shugo Chara Chan!!
Coloring Corner ★
Make a photocopy and
color in the characters!
What will yours look like?

AFTERWORD

This was the third volume of "Shugo Chara Chan!" Amazing!

Ran, Miki, and Su, together with their other Guardian Character friends, really got into a lot of trouble, didnt they? ★

We've been happily following the developments in the "Shugo Chara Chan!" world, and we love them! We want to go there! Let us play with you!

Thanks so much to Naphthalene Mizushima-sensei and all the writers for this manga for breathing life into the Guardian Characters and making this volume even more exciting than the original manga! (Really?)

We're looking forward to Volume 4! ♫

PEACH-PIT

Afterword

あとがき

Hello, this is Naphthalene Mizushima!
I'm the artist who draws the small and adorable Guardian Characters!
My Cat, Abu

The truth is, I'm very small myself!
I stopped growing in fifth grade, so I'm probably about the same height as some of you.
Four foot seven

Actually, I think a lot of the artists at Nakayoshi are pretty short...
Around 4'9"
They're all so cute!

My husband is 5'9", so that makes short people seem even cuter to me!
ゴゴゴゴゴ
LOOM
We're like a couple out of a manga.
So why aren't I cute?

Everyday life for Naphthalene…

I need a stool for everything I do.

For getting utensils

For getting a towel

I can't reach the handles on the train.

My fingers... just barely reach...

プル WOBBLE

プル WOBBLE

I can't open bottle caps.

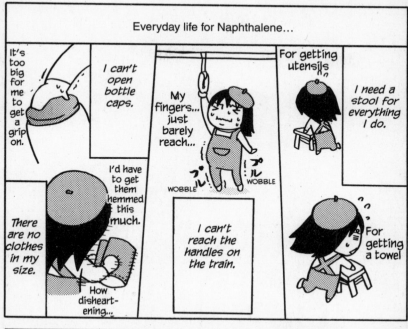

It's too big for me to get a grip on.

There are no clothes in my size.

I'd have to get them hemmed this much.

How disheartening...

While it's not quite the same scale, I'm like a real-life version of the Guardian Characters.
Depiction
I can't fly, though.

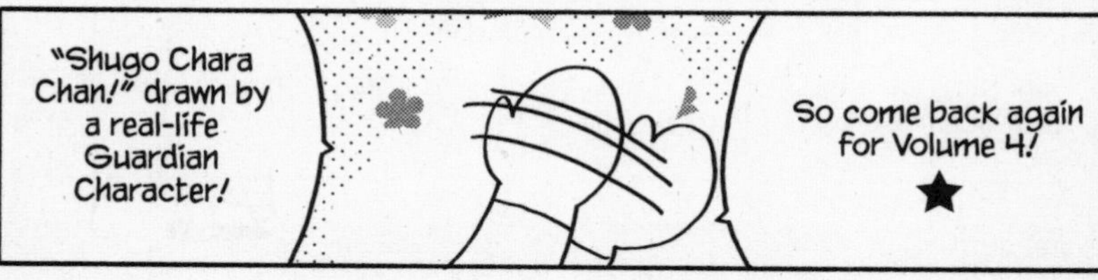
"Shugo Chara Chan!" drawn by a real-life Guardian Character!
So come back again for Volume 4! ★

SHOCKING KC INFORMATION AGAIN
AN IMPORTANT ANNOUNCEMENT FROM DAIYA!
IT'S FINAL!!
"SHUGO CHARA CHAN!" IS COMING BACK IN VOLUME 4!!
Volume 4 already, huh?
What kind of pose should we do for the cover...?
Don't be silly.
TA-DA
Daiya !?
What's with the VIP sun-glasses!?
Since it will be the final cover...
...it needs to be more glamor-ous than ever!!!
She's going to try to crash the cover!!!
Keep your eyes peeled for the result.
VOLUME 4, ON SALE SUMMER 2012

AMU-CHAN AND "SHUGO CHARA CHAN!" VOLUME 4

1

LURCH

Eeek! I'm so excited about Volume 4...

I can't sleep!!

2

Don't worry Amu-chan!

Huh?

3

The path of the stars...

...can cut through time and space.

4

Come! Take the path of the stars to the release date of the manga!

Um...

えっと...

You're not sup-posed to use your magic like that!!

** Kids, please don't cheat! Wait for the release date!*

Thanks to everyone for reading this far!
It's because of your support that we can have a Volume 4! Looking forward to it!!

"SHUGO CHARA CHAN!"

bout The Creators

ACH-PIT:

nri Sendo and Shibuko Ebara

'n June 7 and June 21, respectively. They are a pair of Gemini Manga artists working ether. Currently running "Shugo Chara!" in "Nakayoshi."

phthalene Mizushima

'n February 2. Aquarius. Currently running "Shugo Chara Chan!" in "Nakayoshi."

Translation Notes

Japanese is a tricky language for most Westerners, and translation is often more art than science. For your edification and reading pleasure, here are notes on some of the places where we could have gone in a different direction with our translation of the work, or where a Japanese cultural reference is used.

Giving chocolates on Valentine's Day, pages 37 & 40

In Japan, there is a tradition on Valentines for girls to give chocolates to the boys that they like. But people also give chocolates to their friends or co-workers, so that's why Amu-chan received chocolates from her friends at school! Boys are supposed to pay back the favor on White Day in March.

PREVIEW OF

Shugo Chara Chan!

VOLUME 4

WE'RE PLEASED TO PRESENT YOU A PREVIEW FROM SHUGO CHARA CHAN, VOLUME 4.

PLEASE CHECK OUR WEBSITE (WWW.KODANSHACOMICS.COM) TO SEE WHEN THIS VOLUME WILL BE AVAILABLE IN ENGLISH.

FOR NOW, YOU'LL HAVE TO MAKE DO WITH JAPANESE!

ナフタレン水嶋
しゅごキャラちゃん!
名探偵参上!
事件ですう〜〜
どしたの!?
おととい焼いたマフィンがおいしくできたので また みんなと食べようとのこしといたのに
なくなってたんです!!
思いあたる人は?
いません〜〜
あやしい人は?
じぃ〜
食いしんぼうだからってうたがわないでくださいっっ

太るよ～

みんなのアリバイをききますよ
この二日間なにをしていたか
わあっ
探偵っぽい

二日前は～ お昼に公園であそんで
夕方は おうちのまわりをおさんぽ そのあとは――

ボクは 美術館にいってたよ 帰ってからは 絵を描きつづけた
スゥは？

朝ごはんのあと 二度寝して 十時のおやつに 昼ごはん お昼寝のあと 三時のおやつ…
食っちゃ寝しすぎ!!

かたちから

犯人がなにか証拠を残してるかもですね
このお皿にマフィンをおいてたのです

コレでよ～く調べましょう！
ルーペだ

でも ボクたち 小さいから コレ使わなくても よく見えるのに…
なぜ？

かっこいいからにきまってるじゃないですか!!
あ そう…

作っちゃったよ

こうなったら
おとり作戦です!

まずマフィンを
作って用意して

陰からだれか盗みに
くるのをまつ!
………

イヤ もうそれ自分で
食べればいいじゃん
もう 犯人
どーでもよくない?

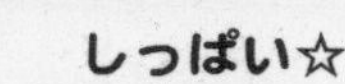
しっぱい☆

犯人をみつけるコトに
イミがあるんです!!
そーですか…

フフ…コレが
はりこみって
やつですね

はりこみといえば
アンパンと
牛乳♡
むぐ

…おなかいっぱいで
眠いですう~……
むにゃ…
むいてないね…

ようぎしゃ

ブブブ

プーーーン

犯人は おまえだ〜〜〜〜!!

いや…ちがうでしょ さすがに食べきれないよね〜

解決!

最後は…ききこみ調査だ! あむちゃんも協力して
あたしたちの声がきこえない人もいるし
いいよーー

カビはえてたから すてたわよ〜〜

梅雨どきは 気をつけなきゃね

………

犯人は ママさん…というか カビでした☆

ちゃんちゃん

なんだったんでしょう… いままでの スゥ……

しく しく…

しゅごキャラちゃん!
ちっちゃなももたろう
初夏だね!
おいしいやさいやくだものがとれるきせつだし
みんなでももたろうごっこやろうよ!
そーっとだなあ
ももはまだ旬じゃないですけどね…
見た目的にもももたろうに近いのは…
やっぱムサシだよね～
む?
でもメガネが…
外しちゃえ♪
うわっ古典的なメガネキャラだ～!
ベタすぎっ
メガネメガネ

人数合わせ
家来は どうする？
だれも やりたくないよ～
そりゃ ちびっこトリオに きまってんじゃん

ちょうど三びきだし！

え～～!!

ぴきっていうな～

確かに ちょうどだけど!!

じゃあ そっち だって…

二人セットの じじばばで 決定だ！

うっ… こっちも イヤだ!! エルまだ ピチピチ なのに～です！

イメージ

三びきの配役どうする？

ランはイヌってカンジです！
そうだな

え？
なんで？

棒をなげると喜んでとってきそうなイメージだから！
うはっ♡
どんなイメージだよ!!

新しい家来

イヌ
サル
キジ

そしてオイラ！
いやネコはいないよ
おはなしに

なんだとーネコだって役立つニャよっ
なにができるんですか～

いやし！
ゴロにゃん
いらね。

そうと聞けば

主人公なのに ももたろう やりたい人いないの？

せっしゃメガネがないとムリでござる

だって 男の子だしー…

とある地方では女の子説があるんだよ
へぇ――

生まれてきた女の子があまりにもかわいいから

鬼にさらわれないように「ももたろう」って名付けたんだって

美少女ってコトですね!! じゃあ エルの出番です!
アタシでしょ!
わたくしですって!

ピンクのおしり

色的に ぺぺは？

ぺぺは めだつのは ちょっと…

でも この色を生かして――
くりん

モモ役で!
ちょこん。
プリッ
かわい♡

ANIMAL LAND

BY MAKOTO RAIKU

In a world of animals, where the strong eat the weak, Monoko the tanuki stumbles across a strange creature the likes of which has never been seen before–a human baby! While the newborn has no claws or teeth to protect itself, it does have the special ability to speak to and understand all different animals. Can the gift of speech between species change the balance of power in a land where the weak must always fear the strong?

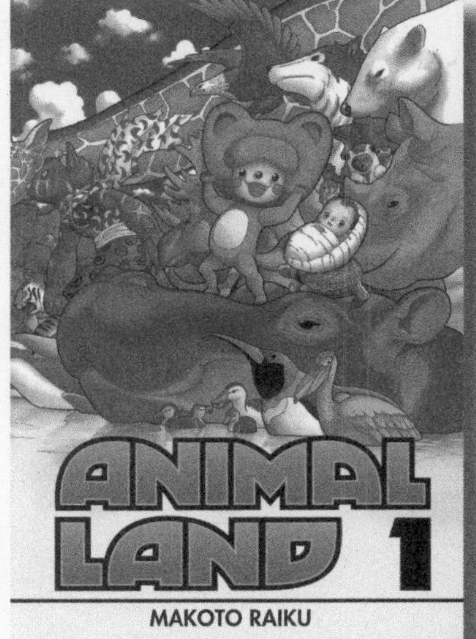
ANIMAL LAND 1
MAKOTO RAIKU

Ages 13+

KC
KODANSHA COMICS

VISIT KODANSHACOMICS.COM TO:

- View release date calendars for upcoming volumes
- Find out the latest about upcoming Kodansha Comics series

4
Pretty Guardian
Sailor Moon
NAOKO
TAKEUCHI

5
Pretty Guardian
Sailor Moon
NAOKO
TAKEUCHI

6
Pretty Guardian
Sailor Moon
NAOKO
TAKEUCHI

NAOKO
TAKEUCHI
7
Pretty Guardian
Sailor Moon

8
Sailor Moon
NAOKO
TAKEUCHI

Sailor Moon
NAOKO
TAKEUCHI

10
Sailor Moon
NAOKO
TAKEUCHI

11
Pretty Guardian
Sailor Moon
NAOKO
TAKEUCHI

12
Sailor Moon
NAOKO
TAKEUCHI

KC
KODANSHA
COMICS